FACTORY
Through the Ages

PHILIP STEELE

Illustrated by
**IVAN LAPPER, ANDREW HOWAT and
GORDON DAVIDSON**

Troll Associates

Library of Congress Cataloging-in-Publication Data

Steele, Philip
    Factory through the ages / by Philip Steele, illustrated by Ivan
Lapper, Andrew Howat and Gordon Davidson
    p.   cm
    Summary: Traces the development of manufacturing in Europe from
the simple process of making axes in ancient times to the
sophisticated factories that exist today.
    ISBN 0-8167-2729-5 (lib. bdg.)   ISBN 0-8167-2730-9 (pbk.)
    1. Factory system–History–Juvenile literature.   2. Factories–
History–Juvenile literature.   3. Labor–History–Juvenile
literature.   4. Working class–History–Juvenile literature.
[1. Factories–History.   2. Manufactures.]   I. Lapper, Ivan, ill.
II. Howat, Andrew, ill.   III. Davidson, Gordon, ill.   IV. Title.
HD2350.8.S74   1993
338.4'767'09–dc20   91–33262

Published by Troll Associates
© 1994 Eagle Books

Design by James Marks

Printed in the U.S.A.

10 9 8 7 6 5 4 3 2 1

Introduction

Humans are creative, busy creatures. The first people played with sticks and stones and found ways to make use of them. They learned how to fashion hunting weapons and fishhooks of bone. They cut sticks for digging and plowing as they began to farm the land. They chipped stone, shaped clay, and eventually learned the secrets of working metal.

Humans became very skilled at manufacturing — the art of making things. They traded their goods with people in other lands. They invented ingenious machines and ways of powering them. In the 1800s, huge cities were built around factories and mills. Chimneys belched smoke and machines hammered day and night.

This story is set in western Europe, and it tells how industry developed there through the ages. But the story belongs to the whole human race, because inventions have come from all over the world.

Contents

The workers selected
and graded the rocks,
splitting them to size
and roughly shaping
them. They chanted
as they worked. In the
summer, the sweat
ran into their eyes. In
the winter, their hands
were chapped from
the cold.

4

Stoneworkers

Stone was this region's greatest resource. Other regions had fine forests or rich, fertile soil. Here there were only bleak moors and low, gray mountains. For thousands of years, rock from these mountains had been chipped and flaked to make axes, spears, and knives. Each generation had its expert workers who hammered stone and worked the surfaces with a fine point until they were razor sharp.

By 2600 B.C. several villages had grown up in the valley. Each dawn, groups of workers set out and returned carrying baskets of stones. By firelight they finished the axheads, grinding and polishing them, carefully testing the blades with their thumbs.

Each spring, traders sailed down the coast. Because of the traders, the local stone was known even in distant regions. The villagers exchanged the axes for pots, necklaces, and bone harpoons. This year the traders had a special gift for the chief. It was a knife that had been made far away to the south. It was made of copper, smooth and straight, and it glinted in the firelight.

The secret of bronze

The smoke from the furnaces billowed across the valley and hung over the village all summer long. Copper had been found in the inland mountains. The mining gangs now filled one basket after another with ore— the rocks that contained the precious metal. Carriers brought the ore down from the peaks.

Potters had first learned how to build furnaces to fire and harden their clay dishes. Metalworkers needed even higher temperatures. Bronze melts at over 1,600°F (900°C). The precious alloy was poured into molds cut from blocks of stone. The mold was greased with a sooty mixture, filled with bronze, and then covered. When the bronze had cooled and hardened, the mold was broken open.

By 1600 B.C., the traders' ships brought an even more precious metal. This was tin, mined far away in the southwest. The ores were melted down, or *smelted*, in the glowing furnaces, so that the metals were separated from the impurities in the ore. One part of tin was mixed with up to nine parts of copper. The molten mixture, or alloy, was called bronze.

The secret of bronze working had long been known in the cities of the east. The new metal was hard and tough. It could be hammered, ground, and polished. It was fashioned into tools, pins, axes, spearheads, daggers, helmets, and shields. It was used to make earrings for the chief's daughter.

7

Celtic ironworkers

Different people had come and gone. In 500 B.C. the Celts brought with them the secret of working iron, a skill learned from other people. Iron was a harder metal than copper or bronze. The people who lived in the northern forests thought it was magic, made by spirits or gods. In fact, it was smelted in huge furnaces fanned by bellows.

Iron was used to make swords, spearheads, sickles, tongs, and wheel rims for chariots. Bronze was still used for all kinds of tools and weapons, and could be polished to make fine hand mirrors. Silver and gold were fashioned into dazzling ornaments.

No one could work metal like the Celts. It was twisted and hammered into the shape of human figures, birds, horses, and stags. These designs decorated the caldrons that bubbled over the cooking fires in the Celts' huts.

Iron was heated until it glowed, and then was hammered into shape. The finished piece was plunged into water. The iron sizzled and steamed as it cooled.

Roman potteries

The Romans invaded the region in A.D. 50. They wanted to control the copper mines and quarry the local stone. Many of the Celts were forced into hard labor by their new masters. There were many revolts, but by A.D. 200 the region was peaceful and prosperous.

To the south of the mountains there was a belt of heavy, sticky soil that was hard to plow. This was clay, and though it may not have been ideal for farming, it was perfect for pottery.

A wealthy Roman set up a workshop there that employed over 30 local people as potters and laborers.

The finished red clayware was stored in stacks. The owner of the pottery boasted that his warehouse could hold 500,000 items.

Many Romans said that the pottery back home was of a superior quality. However, when the wife of the new Roman governor placed an order for this locally made ware, many others followed her. The pottery was placed in crates, packed with straw, and exported by land and sea.

The master potters worked the wheels, wetting, shaping, and curving the clay. Others worked with molds, decorating bowls and pots with hunting scenes and leaf patterns. The trademark of the pottery was stamped into the soft clay. Then the pottery was loaded into kilns, where it was fired until hard.

Power from water

There was fighting in distant lands. Rome was sacked in A.D. 410 and Roman legions were no longer seen in these remote parts. Stone was no longer quarried in the mountains. Weeds grew in the courtyard of the ironworks. The old pottery sheds were broken up for firewood. Savage warriors raided the lowland valleys each spring.

Trade was poor. The roads became rutted, and wagons of goods were often seized by bandits. Manufacturing was carried out in local cottages by peasants and their families. The rest of the world was passing Europe by. However, Europeans were making good use of one important resource—water.

In the past, teams of oxen or slave gangs had done the hard work. Now water wheels provided mechanical power. Water power was eventually used for all kinds of industry, from metalwork to sawing timber.

The Romans had used water wheels as early as 70 B.C. for grinding wheat and pressing the oil from olives. Some were directly powered by the current. With others, a chute dropped water onto the top of the wheel. The main wheel turned other wheels and drove the machinery.

In the year 900, the lord of the valley built a new water mill. He sent out his soldiers to break up all the stone hand mills that the peasants had always used for grinding grain. Now everyone had to use the water mill and the lord became rich on the proceeds.

The glass blowers

These were troubled times. The plague had killed many local people, and workers became scarce. When they demanded better pay, laws were introduced to control wages. The peasants rose up and burned down the castle at the head of the valley. Soldiers came to restore order, and punishment was harsh and swift.

The year 1400, however, was fairly peaceful. The weaving workshops in the growing town provided a trade for many, and woolen cloth was a major export.

The best glass was made in the Italian city of Venice. But a local

Venetian glass was made from a mixture of sand, soda, and lime. This mixture was melted in glowing furnaces.

manufacturer learned the skills and set up his own glassworks in the town. They made drinking glasses, as well as stained glass for the new church.

14

Weavers, glass blowers, and other manufacturers set up trade associations called guilds. These controlled the quality of goods and fixed prices. The guilds also trained young boys as apprentices. It could take up to seven years for them to qualify for the guild.

Drinking glasses were shaped by blowing the molten glass through a long iron pipe. The bubble grew into a fine, round bulb. Other shapes were produced by spinning, twisting, and stretching the molten glass.

Shipbuilding

This western coast had once been a remote region isolated from the rest of the world. Now that ships were sailing to the Americas, however, its position on the Atlantic Ocean made it an important trade center. Many families sailed away to colonies in the New World. Galleons returned laden with gold, silver, tobacco leaf, and strange plants, such as potatoes. Other ships were setting sail for the East Indies in search of exotic spices.

Ships were built by the power of human muscle. Carpenters constructed a huge framework of oak timbers. They fastened planks to the outside of the shell. Three or four tall masts were fitted and rigged with sails.

By 1620 a large port had grown up, with yards for building and refitting ocean-going ships. The shipyards were a hive of activity. Shipwrights discussed plans of the vessels with captains and merchants. Carpenters hammered and sawed.

16

Shipwrights knew how the timbers would swell when soaked in water. They learned to make strong joints and secured them with wooden pegs. Caldrons of black, sticky pitch bubbled and smoked. Pitch and rope fiber were used for sealing joints to make the ship watertight.

Shipbuilding provided work for many kinds of trades. Sail makers stitched canvas to make the huge sails. Rope makers prepared the rigging and the mooring lines. Iron foundries produced anchors and cannons, which merchant ships needed for protection against foreign naval vessels and pirates. Onlookers sat on the sea wall and watched the work in progress. Children dreamed of exciting adventures at sea.

A new industrial age

Until the 1700s, industry was powered by humans, animals, wind, or water. Then steam engines were invented. Water was turned into steam inside a boiler. The steam passed into a cylinder where it was condensed into water once more. The change in pressure forced a piston to move, and this movement was transferred to beams and rods. Steam engines were first used to operate water pumps in coal and tin mines.

This was a new industrial age. Iron was smelted in hot, glowing furnaces. Canals were dug across the landscape. Large "manufactories" were built to make pottery. By the early 1800s, large cities were growing up around such "factories." Smoke from tall chimneys blackened the buildings.

The weaving industry saw many rapid changes. The machines that spun the yarn and the looms that made the cloth were made to go faster and faster. Hand weavers and spinners could not compete with these new machines, and many people lost their jobs. Some attacked the workshops and smashed the hated power looms. Water power gave way to steam power in the textile mills, and cotton was imported to make cheap, light cloth.

Working conditions in the textile mill were hard. Women and children worked twelve-hour shifts, night and day. Pay was low and the housing, which had to be rented from the factory owner, was poorly built.

1830 was a busy year for this textile mill. Bales of cotton were unloaded at the port and ferried by canal to the mill. The finished cotton cloth was sent all over the country and overseas.

The coming of the railroads

The factories needed a new system of transportation so that coal, machinery, and goods could be moved long distances at fast speeds. Railroad trains had been developed in Great Britain between 1804 and 1813. They were powered by high-pressure steam. Soon new railroads were being built across western Europe and North America.

In 1850 a new railroad was opened between the port and the growing cities to the east. The railroad cars and the iron locomotives that hauled them were assembled at a new engineering works, which employed many men.

The sheds were noisy places, full of clanking, screeching, and hammering. Pulleys and chains rattled and rumbled. The smell of oil hung in the air.

The finished locomotives had long, horizontal boilers with high chimneys. They were coupled with tenders, which carried water and coal for the firebox. As the locomotives were driven out to the yards, steam hissed and billowed across the tracks.

The man who designed the locomotives was the railroad company's chief engineer. He had many problems to solve. Which was the best gauge, or track width? Which was the safest design? Which was the fastest? Which wheels would keep the train securely on the tracks?

The works was at its busiest between 1850 and 1860, as thousands of miles of track were laid across the country. A large town grew up around the works.

The long section of the boiler was called the barrel. It was made of iron. The water was heated by thin tubes leading from a copper firebox. As the water became hot, it turned to steam. The pressure of the steam moved pistons that were connected to the wheels.

The steelworks

Industry relied on iron. Wrought iron, which could be hammered or rolled into shape, was now used to make bridges, railway tracks, and steamship hulls. Cast iron, melted in blast furnaces at a very high temperature, could not be reworked and was used to make machine parts.

The steel was made into large bars called ingots. These could be rolled into flat plates for shipbuilding or forged into rails or locomotive parts. Steel girders were used as a framework for buildings and bridges.

Iron needed to be toughened. For centuries people had tried to make "steel" by controlling the amount of carbon in the iron. But the process was slow and expensive. It was only used when making swords or knives.

A British inventor named Henry Bessemer and an American named William Kelly both found a way of making large quantities of steel cheaply. Cold air was blown through molten iron. This purified the iron by getting rid of the naturally occurring carbon and silicon. A carefully measured amount of carbon was then added to harden the mixture, making high-quality steel.

A huge steelworks was built on the edge of the city in 1870. A branch of the railroad was built to carry iron ore to the furnaces and finished steel from the works.

Work in the steel mill was hard, hot, and often dangerous. Accidents were common. The workers asked the owner for better working conditions and higher wages. They formed a labor union to protect their rights.

Making cars

Industry saw more changes in the 19th century than it had in the previous 2,000 years. Natural gas was piped for heating and lighting. Chemicals were developed for making dyes and treating rubber. Machines could now be powered by electricity. The first gasoline-powered car took to the road in Germany in 1885.

In 1900, a mechanic set up a small garage in the city. He experimented with designs for motorcyles and cars. He and his friends formed a company that made cars. Each one was carefully made and very expensive.

By 1930, the company had grown large. It occupied a busy factory on the edge of the city. The manufacturer built cars according to a system developed in the United States by Henry Ford. The cars were passed along an assembly line. Each worker carried out a single job at each stage of production. The finished cars were cheap, and thousands were sold.

The cars passed slowly along a moving belt. Each part was mass-produced. It took little more than three working hours to complete a car.

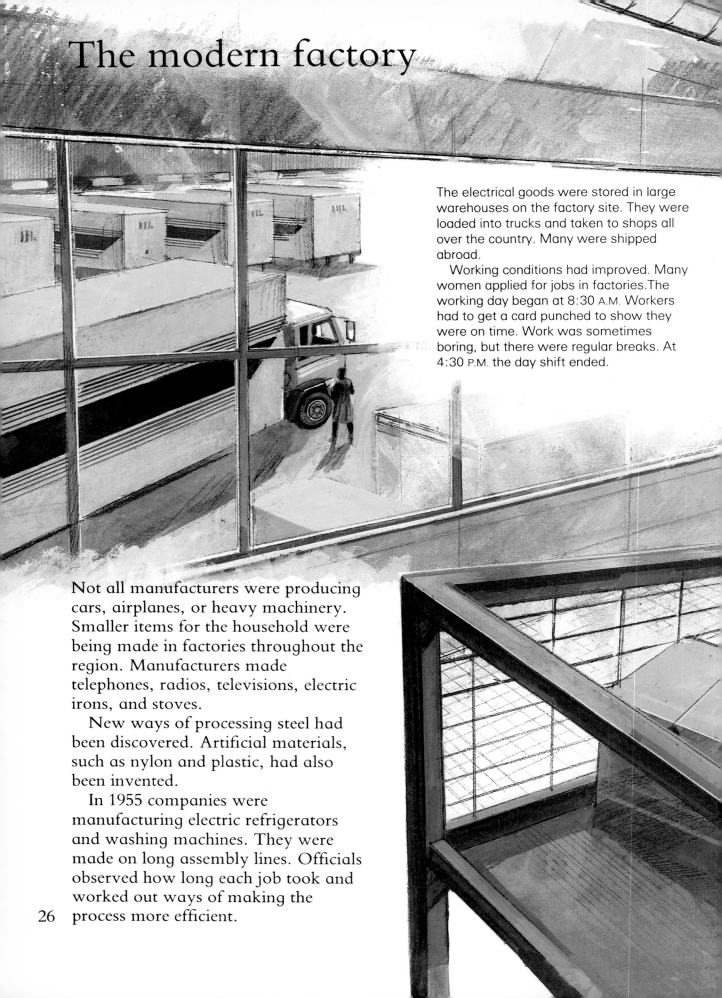

The modern factory

The electrical goods were stored in large warehouses on the factory site. They were loaded into trucks and taken to shops all over the country. Many were shipped abroad.

Working conditions had improved. Many women applied for jobs in factories. The working day began at 8:30 A.M. Workers had to get a card punched to show they were on time. Work was sometimes boring, but there were regular breaks. At 4:30 P.M. the day shift ended.

Not all manufacturers were producing cars, airplanes, or heavy machinery. Smaller items for the household were being made in factories throughout the region. Manufacturers made telephones, radios, televisions, electric irons, and stoves.

New ways of processing steel had been discovered. Artificial materials, such as nylon and plastic, had also been invented.

In 1955 companies were manufacturing electric refrigerators and washing machines. They were made on long assembly lines. Officials observed how long each job took and worked out ways of making the process more efficient.

The finished machines were tested to make sure that everything worked well. The electrical wiring had to be safe. The surface paint had to resist scratching and had to protect the metal from rust. The company controlled the quality of goods very carefully.

The machines were advertised in the newspapers and on television. Their brand names became known in every household. Sales grew year by year.

27

The present

The old cotton mill was demolished in 1985 because cheaper textiles were now produced overseas. The steelworks closed in 1988 because fewer ships and railways were being built. A new factory was built on the site. It was owned by a Japanese firm that manufactured computers.

The new firm employed both women and men. Precision and accuracy were needed for this work. Many routine jobs were carried out by electronic machines known as robots. These were programmed to carry out tasks on the assembly line.

Computers had been developed in Great Britain and the United States. The first machines went on sale in the early 1950s. They were huge, with large banks of wires. In the 1950s and 1960s, ways were found to make computers smaller. By 1975, personal computers were being produced for home and office. They could be used for word processing, calculation, storing records, industrial design, or playing games.

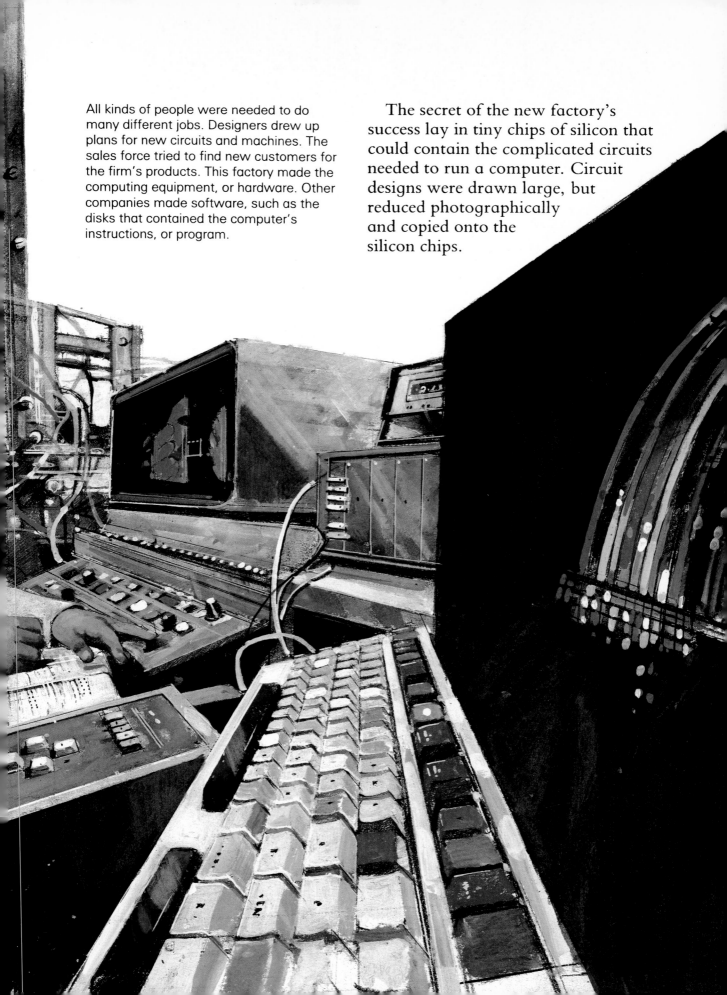

All kinds of people were needed to do many different jobs. Designers drew up plans for new circuits and machines. The sales force tried to find new customers for the firm's products. This factory made the computing equipment, or hardware. Other companies made software, such as the disks that contained the computer's instructions, or program.

The secret of the new factory's success lay in tiny chips of silicon that could contain the complicated circuits needed to run a computer. Circuit designs were drawn large, but reduced photographically and copied onto the silicon chips.

The future

Had human beings been too clever for their own good? Two thousand years had seen the region turn from wild countryside into a landscape of paved roads and tall buildings.

Forests had been cut down to build ships and supply fuel for furnaces. Iron, copper, oil, and coal had been taken from the ground and used. They could not last forever.

In the early 1990s, chemical waste from factories was still killing fish in the rivers. Smoke and exhaust fumes in the air were forming acid rain. Whole lakes lay poisoned and lifeless.

People could not stop making things. Many now depended on manufacturing in order to stay alive. Scientists were looking for new solutions to the problems.

Industry was wasteful, so they studied new ways of saving energy. Factory waste and smoke were to be more strictly controlled. Cars were developed that could run on the power of the sun. New fuels that would not pollute the air, such as hydrogen, were developed.

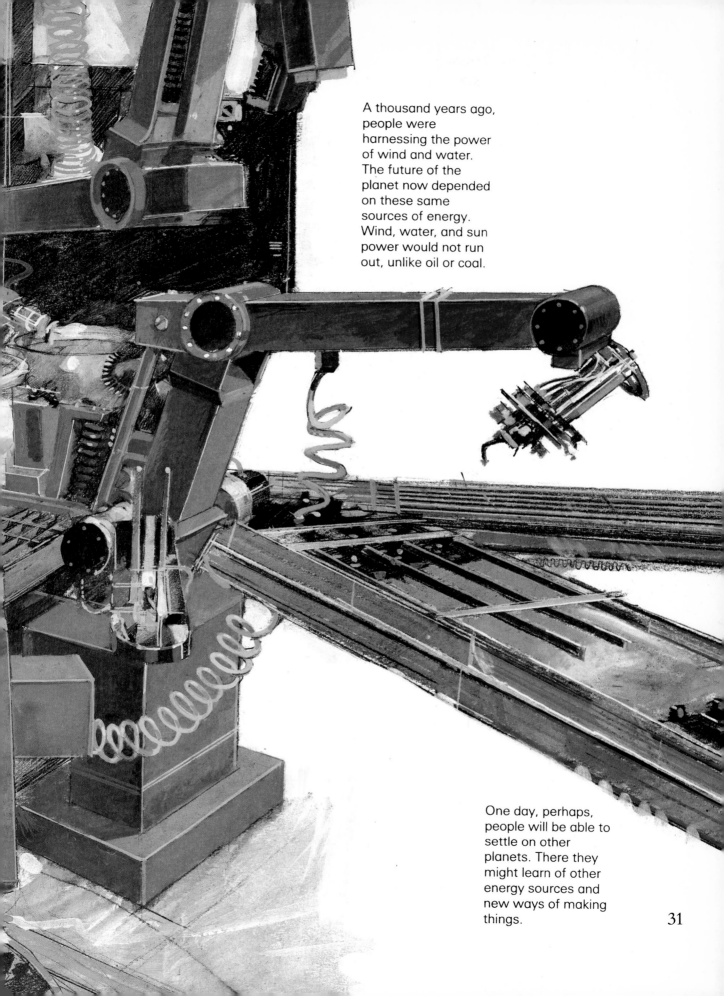

A thousand years ago, people were harnessing the power of wind and water. The future of the planet now depended on these same sources of energy. Wind, water, and sun power would not run out, unlike oil or coal.

One day, perhaps, people will be able to settle on other planets. There they might learn of other energy sources and new ways of making things.

Index